≈§ In Sepia

Jon Anderson

In Sepia

University of Pittsburgh Press

Library of Congress Cataloging in Publication Data

Anderson, Jon.

In sepia.

(Pitt poetry series)

I. Title.

PS3551.N3715   1974   811'.5'4   73–13310
ISBN 0–8229–3278–4
ISBN 0–8229–5245–9 (pbk.)

Acknowledgment is made to the following publications in which some of these poems first appeared: *Back Door, Field, The Iowa Review, Lotus,* and *Ohio Review.*

"Exile," "In Sepia," "Level," and "The Inner Gate" were first published in *Poetry.*

Notes:
The quotation in "The Journey from Essex" is from John Clare's journal of his escape from High Beech Asylum. In fact, unguarded & allowed to wander at will in the woods bordering the asylum, Clare simply decided to go home.

In "Poems from the Chinese," while no substantial changes have been made in the imagery of each, many lines have been omitted or rearranged, sometimes entirely altering the emotive intention of the original. This was done to personalize the poems, meant to be read as a sequence. The poets are, in order: Meng Hao-jan, Tu Fu, three by Wang Wei, Meng Hao-jan again, Wen T'ing-yun, & Wang Wei again.

The first line of the third section of "Stories" is from Rilke's poem, "People by Night."

for The Grommit

Grommits are cute,
Grommits are nice;
Kiss them once,
Kiss them twice!

—T. Dwarf

CONTENTS

The place we occupy seems all the world.
—John Clare, "November"

John Clare

I know there is a worm in the human heart,
In its wake such emptiness as sleep should require.

Toward dawn, there was an undirected light the color of steel;
The aspens, thin, vaguely parallel strips of slate,
Blew across each other in that light.
                                        I went out
Having all night suffered my confusion, &
Was quieted by this.
                        But the earth
Vegetable rock or water that had been our salvation
Is mostly passed now, into the keeping of John Clare,
Alive,
        whose poetry simplified us—we owe the world ourselves—
Who, dead or sleeping, now reads the detail leaf & stone
Passing, until it will finally be memorized & done.

I know the heart can be hard, & from this
Misgiving about itself, will make a man merciless.
I know that John Clare's madness nature could not straighten.

If there is a worm in the heart, & chamber it has bitten out,
I will protect that emptiness until it is large enough.
In it will be a light the color of steel
& landscape, into which the traveler might set out.

Rosebud

There is a place in Montana where the grass stands up two feet,
Yellow grass, white grass, the wind
On it like locust wings & the same shine.
Facing what I think was south, I could see a broad valley
& river, miles into the valley, that looked black & then trees.
To the west was more prairie, darker
Than where we stood, because the clouds
Covered it; a long shadow, like the edge of rain, racing toward us.
We had been driving all day, & the day before through South Dakota
Along the Rosebud, where the Sioux
Are now farmers, & go to school, & look like everyone.
In the reservation town there was a Sioux museum
& 'trading post', some implements inside: a longbow
Of shined wood that lay in its glass case, reflecting light.
The walls were covered with framed photographs,
The Oglala posed in fine dress in front of a few huts,
Some horses nearby: a feeling, even in those photographs
The size of a book, of spaciousness.
I wanted to ask about a Sioux holy man, whose life
I had recently read, & whose vision had gone on hopelessly
Past its time: I believed then that only a great loss
Could make us feel small enough to begin again.
The woman behind the counter
Talked endlessly on; there was no difference I could see
Between us, so I never asked.

The place in Montana
Was the *Greasy Grass* where Custer & the Seventh Cavalry fell,
A last important victory for the tribes. We had been driving
All day, hypnotized, & when we got out to enter
The small, flat American tourist center we began to argue.
And later, walking between the dry grass & reading plaques,
My wife made an ironic comment: I believe it hurt the land, not
Intentionally; it was only meant to hold us apart.
Later I read of Benteen & Ross & those who escaped,
But what I felt then was final: lying down, face
Against the warm side of a horse, & feeling the lulls endlessly,
The silences just before death. The place might stand for death,
Every loss rejoined in a wide place;
Or it is rest, as it was after the long drive,
Nothing for miles but grass, a long valley to the south
& living in history. Or it is just a way of living
Gone, like our own, every moment.
Because what I have to do daily & what is done to me
Are a number of small indignities, I have to trust that
Many things we all say to each other are not intentional,
That every indirect word will accumulate
Over the earth, & now, when we may be approaching
Something final, it seems important not to hurt the land.

A Commitment

After I watched your face, behind its mask
Of talk, deaden, then grow animate,
Alternating light & dark as you bowed
& drew yourself erect under the lamplight
Of someone else's room in which we talked,
I was restored. Though in the minor
Darkness of my heart, where I'm most alone,
I wanted to take your masculine face
Between my hands & press for strength.
The skull, for me, is death & strength,
Merely objective in a world of sense.

Within a month you lost your wife & friend.
But not to death. I knew their leaving
Had the appearance of a judgment on your life.
Because the friend was also mine & gone,
Because I loved your wife, in you or apart,
And because you wouldn't turn aside, I tilted
The lampshade down & drifted with you
On the edge of dark.

                  I remembered an evening
With friends in a small boat on a lake.
It was September: the late afternoon light
& wine we drank warmed us to each other.
Our quietness then passed from the shadows
Of trees close to the water—it seemed
We had drifted out over a great emptiness,
Silent, held only by our composure . . .

I think, now, of those friends: I
Let them go. Really, only for the ease
Of letting go. Now when I visit & attend
Their lives, they are partly strange; I know
My hesitations seem to judge their house.

I wanted to say, as I watched you steady
Yourself in the dark, I was restored
By your bearing & openness to pain,
A commitment to what you had already lost.
Our talk was personal; I said it in another way.

But if all our losses are a form of death,
A mirror in which we see ourselves advance,
I believe in its terrible, empty reflection,
Its progress from judgment toward compassion.

7

The Journey from Essex, July 1841

At age 48, being of unsound mind,
Removed by his own volition from public life,
Escaped July 18, High Beech Epping Asylum,
Walking six days with little food, few words
Spoken only to strangers, to beg
Directions & some bread, arrived:
So here I am homeless at home & half
Gratified to be anywhere.

—John Clare

Removed again to Northampton (December)
Where he died,
Though for twenty-five years there
Was allowed some kindness,
Encouragement of his verse
& some small land on which to garden.

*

Kindly kept prisoner those hundred seasons,
Aware of the heart's affection for dark misguidance,
Failed of marriage & ambition,
Please John Clare, there was time
To put consequence aside & set out for home again.
Because your poetry simplifies us
We are the earth's innocence,
Alone, in no one's care . . .

John Clare,
So you may stay at home,
I will try to hold back some harshness.
Nor judge myself continually, or any man.

Ye Bruthers Dogg

Hodain D. Dogg
& Toolie Orlen

Ye dogg, O'Toole,
Who hath not work
At love nor arte
Nor goeth schule
Sayeth with fart
At Gulden Rulle,
"Be it bitch or bisquit
Or platter stewe,
Ye palate alone shal guide yu."

Ye dogg, Hodain,
Forgoeth bone
Nor doth distain
To moanne,
". . . for winde & raen,
Ye snow & fogg,
Ye seasons, sunn,
& world roll on,
But ye dayes a' dogg be not longe."

Bruthers Tew,
Ye slimm Hodain
& fatte O'Toole,
Beneath fense
Diggeth hole.
Into ye world
Ye Bruthers danse;
Nor wuld return
Ye fatte O'Toole & slimm Hodain.

Sune is report
Bruthers Tew
Doth run amok
I' neighborhude.
Cautions O'Toole,
"Hodain, ye may barke,
May scowle & be rude,
But do not bitte
Ye hand what giveth dogg fude."

Tho all complane
A' Bruthers Tew,
No winde nor raen
Doth drive them homme.
Then sayeth Hodain
To Bruther, "O'Toole,
Tho we hath been frende
Thru thik & thinn,
Dogg needeth sume love from Mann."

So ende ye song
A' Bruthers Tew.
Away they had flown
& back they flewe.
Reclineth i' yard
Thru seasons & sunn,
Thru winde & raen,
Ye snow, ye fogg,
O'Toole, Hodain, ye Bruthers Dogg.

Poems from the Chinese

How could I oversleep this spring morning?
The music of birds surrounds my awakening.

Then I remember last night's wind & rain,
How many blossoms have fallen while I slept.

*

Far from the city, I lean on an open porch.
An occasional tree bows with its summer weight.
The dogs run in circles snapping at flies,
Fish rise in the river to nibble at raindrops.

Ten thousand families in that far city
But here—only two or three small homes.

*

As I've grown older, I've taken to solitude.
I wonder what ambition brought me here.

I walk in the chill, forgetting to button my coat,
& sometimes by moonlight mutter to no one.

You ask me why my life is such confusion!

*

Even after it rains the hills are dry.
The moon catches in pine branches
& in the evening we feel a touch of autumn.

The stream is so clear now stones seem to float away.
Children going home rattle milkweed stalks.
The fisherman's boat nudges the reeds aside.

Did this spring, again, so casually slip away.

*

Please let's drink one last cup of wine—
When you leave this house, who will be your friend?

*

In the river mist I tied my boat to the bank.
I have a wanderer's sadness at evening.

Here, between earth & heaven, a tree can be lost,
But on the water the moon shines beside me.

*

A few stars,
Mostly silence.
At my window, the morning oriole,
                the narrow moon.
Willows lean in the wind; a few leaves drift.

I find myself
Hesitant at my door:
Everywhere the year's regrets.
                Cares seem to have no end.
Among them, like a dream . . . one remembered joy . . .

*

No one comes to this wilderness,
Only a sound like far-off conversation.

Shadows drift back among the trees.
Again the moss shines green with sunlight.

In Autumn

At day's light
I dressed my cold body & went out.
Calling the dogs, I climbed the west hill,
Threw cut wood down to the road for hauling.
Done, there was a kind of exultation
That wanted to go on; I made my way
Up through briars & vines
To a great stone that rises at the hill's brow,
Large enough to stand on. The river
Below was a thick, dark line.
My house was quaint.
I sat, not thoughtful,
Lost in the body awhile,
Then came down the back way, winding
Through stands of cedar & pine.

I can tell you where I live.
My grief is that I bear no grief
& so I bear myself. I know I live apart.
But have had long evenings of conversation,
The faces of which betrayed
No separation from a place or time. Now,
In the middle of my life,
A woman of delicate bearing gives me
Her hand, & friends
Are so enclosed within my reasoning
I am occasionally them.

When I had finally stood, high above
The house, land, my life's slow dream,
For a moment I was required
To turn to those deep rows of cedar,

& would have gone
On walking endlessly in.
I understand by the body's knowledge
I will not begin again.
But it was October: leaves
In the yellowed light were altered & familiar.
We who have changed, & have
No hope of change, must now love
The passage of time.

Though I Long to Be No One

I passed for two nights
& days, alone,
On a train.

Whatever I do
I am always leaving.
Whoever's face I lay my own along,
The cheekbones bruised & rose.

Faces of friends,
Of women;
The elongated face of my third wife, aged
& concerned about my house . . .

Nightly I carry them forward in sleep,
Though I long to be no one.

The wheels of iron pass
Over these rails
& boards above water.
Over the bodies of my constant departure
Into my constant longing.

The Days

All day I bear myself to such reward:
I close my eyes, I can't sleep,
The trees are whispering flat as water.

My friends' grayed faces
Do not alter with the weather anymore.
We sit by a cold stove & talk.
We suffer the terrible news.

Into a world made over & over
You rise each day,
You remember,
& something goes wrong.

God, if I had a wish, I swear
I wouldn't know what to spend it on.

A Bridge in Fog

Cars at a great distance crossed in a line.
Below, the boats went forward towing their lights.
When I came to myself, I was divided within myself;
Merely for solace, I'd been watching a long time

& was still troubled as I turned toward home.
In its dark windows I could see myself approach,
So suffered my strangeness in reflection.
My wife was asleep. I was glad to be alone.

It was not for the scene I'd stood transfixed,
Only its lights' methodical passage by water,
& above, where the cars' beams flickered in mist . . .

Just before sleep I've traveled awhile like this.

Other Lives

The guest sits in her flowered chair.
She is like a lion,
All muscular potential.

When she leaps, you will die of embarrassment.
You will die of the domestic.
But she never will.

Those other lives,
Hers, everyone's, yours,
Are reserved, even from themselves.

You only fear their essence—
Coming from such distances
It is inscrutable, austere.

And you? . . . unworthy of its coldest glance.

In the mirror, another stares back
Because the face is depthless glass,
Silvered at the brain's back to reflect.

You have given your guest your hand.
Out in the night, she rises like a ghoul
Into the moon's face, laughing.

No, she is just walking to her car,
As you are walking to sleep,
That alabaster sea whose tides the moon controls.

A Woodblock by Hiroshige

They are appearing, one
By one from below
The picture. I wonder

If that narrow
Bridge they cross
Will support their slow

Processional pace,
Which seems
A ritual. They face

Downward in perpetual
Acceptance. Below, the stream
Tosses. If I should call,

Would they hear? The rain
Beats upon their round
Gold hats & runs

Away; the ground
Beneath their feet is running away.
And I call. But the sound

Is lost, indifferent. Now they
Have crossed the narrow
Bridge. They are going away.

I watch them go.
The sound, of the rain,
Of the stream, follows.

Autumn Day

The leaves are falling, the wind blows cold.
This light is nothing. It enters & reflects.
Out of a cloud I came falling into a cloud.
The wind blows & the leaves are falling.

Under the great world's trees I'm walking.
I entered a cloud. It was my name.
I entered a world in which people are walking,
The leaves are falling & the wind blows cold.

April

Lord, yearly
I have not learned,
But meet that early spring
Emptied again of heart.
I have bargained my love
For love of what that first cold
April day foretold:
In your arms is the exquisite pain,
It is your forehead leans,
Not mine. And if I yearn . . .
That is not anything.
For I have sent my loves away
& taken to my loin
Your first cold green & naked day.

Spring Snow

So now it's spring again,
If I live in a spare season
I prefer it so.

Last night's April snow
Came on us unprepared,
I found myself out walking alone.

Alone, I'd watch the snow
Fall down on Massachusetts, where I lived.
I didn't have anything then.

I thought I'd have a son
By now, by someone,
Out of the grace I'd grow.

It was myself I grew:
Starlight, snowfall, cold & dark,
Whatever I want I can outwalk.

I didn't have anything then.
Spring snow, when I can live again,
I'll put myself aside.

So let it fall.

The Secret of Poetry

When I was lonely, I thought of death.
When I thought of death I was lonely.

I suppose this error will continue.
I shall enter each gray morning

Delighted by frost, which is death,
& the trees that stand alone in mist.

When I met my wife I was lonely.
Our child in her body is lonely.

I suppose this error will go on & on.
Mornings I kiss my wife's cold lips,

Nights her body, dripping with mist.
This is the error that fascinates.

I suppose you are secretly lonely,
Thinking of death, thinking of love.

I'd like, please, to leave on your sill
Just one cold flower, whose beauty

Would leave you inconsolable all day.
The secret of poetry is cruelty.

The Inner Gate

At a certain time of my life
That failure I had long before surmised,
Which was a destiny born
Of self-consciousness, assured itself.

I felt I had been walking aimlessly
Between shops & houses, along
Narrow cobbled sidewalks,
Turning corners as they occurred
In a Mediterranean city.

Passing its stained fountains,
Galleries,
Gates behind which were narrow yards
Full of flowers & washing,
I had lost track of memory.

Out of my longing
I had invented this particular city.

Within its heart
A house,
A room,
A diary of aesthetic change.

Though I had seldom mentioned within it
Those events or names by which
I was compelled to write,
I had secretly thought to accrue a life:

To imply
The passage of time.
Of myself, as citizen, from here to here.

*

I became coldly hysterical.
I attempted some small injuries. Scraping
My forearm across the rough stucco of a house front,
My blood speckled it a dull brown,
The color of old tintypes.

This regulated motion enraged me.
Even the pain grew melancholy
With its obsessive pulse.

I thought of picking a fight,
Or entering a shop to bring my fist
Crashing down on its display case:
I saw a hand rising
Through brooches & rings, to meet my hand
In the shadowy glass.

I realized I would remember
Only my conception, not the act.

The man who would beat me was already recognized.

*

Perhaps I was stunned; my mind
Which seemed now to have conceived even itself,
Would not function beyond
A certain repetition:

I saw myself, seated at a desk
In a small room, rise
From writing again & again.
My vision, with each rising of the figure,
Crossed by inches the plain wood floor,
The desk on which a journal
Lay open, toward a window.

The room,
Its furniture & bare white walls,
Lay otherwise in shadow.

I did not know if I was waking, or passing
Deeper into an obsessive dream;
I could see the light, sloped roofs of the city,
& below, a courtyard,
High walled & windowless but for my own.

*

Then I began walking.
I felt the eyes of others watching, as if,
Among these streets,
These pastel storefronts & shades of my making,
I was recognizably foreign.

As I turned corner after corner
My anxiety steadied
To a form of relaxed pursuit.

I found myself following a group of men;
Among them, one
Who in a former life,
Before the nets or mirrors had descended
Upon all motion of history,
I had seen as my future.

That is, in his comfortable,
Terrible submission to the traps of the familiar,
I had seen my own progression.

*

One by one these men dissolved into doorways.
The afternoon grew less hot.

In my singularity of following
I was relieved, & seemed carried
On a small boat down those blue, winding streets,
Often in the shadows of trees.

He turned at the heavy iron gate
Of an alley, touched
His remaining friends' shoulders,
& entered.

*

So I had made my way,
Which was after all by chance, & effortless.

As I passed from gate to inner gate
& into a high-walled yard,
My bitterness ripened. Standing in the flowers
Below his window,
I watched as he ate & read;
I watched the narrow passage of stars
& as his light went out.

If he had stepped outside
I might have strangled him,
Only to see his face fill with blood.

I desired a single, terrible event,
The passage from which would measure time.

*

On a stone bench, beneath a tree,
A man is smoking.
He sits in a patience of shadows
Above which the stars turn slowly.

Now the first wheels rumble
Over cobblestone. An awning
Is lowered.
Shopkeepers shade their faces from the sun.

And if, this morning
I should turn & touch your face
Or caress your throat lightly,
As if in love . . .

This is not love, but care.
Yours is the world
I dream in when I fail to dream.

*

These are the raptures of falling in space forever.

And sometimes, in those solemn hours,
I felt my life already lived and over:
as in old journals, we come upon a story
that seems our own, and speaks, then passes.
  —Rilke, *The Book of Hours*

Counting the Days

Just as we wake up, yawn, & lift a shade to explore,
(Always imperfectly amazed at subtle change, but limited
By expectations & the window's frame from which we gaze;
A yard: of weeds & dogs & brown boughs, though
Sometimes even the boughs are altered by falling snow)

So he is counting the days, the years, back toward
A serious initial thought: that he was *here*,
Was *someone*, was counting the days toward when
He would (today) count back: an important déjà vu.

Accompany him, please. This journey into dissolution
As memories become events, become anticipations,
Then dissolve, will empty us of our complex doubts.
You will certainly love yourselves as history: potential
Which only took a certain lovely, arbitrary route . . .

As on a December afternoon, the stillness of which
Engenders that image of falling snow, we now
Begin again that art our lives become.

Refusals

Sometimes we get down to loneliness
& poetry is just talking about things.
In the wake of those graceful verses,
Those boats loaded with spiced meat & jewels,
Is a silence meant to kill.

                      So you talk
About death; you expel it,
The sweets of dioxide, into the air.
And driving all night, in silence,
You see it flying by.
Is it sweet, that you love it so? You're not
A poor bastard yet; you give some affection . . .
Like alms, or smooth as cheese.

And you still love the loneliness in marriage:
Refusals of sex & shared meals, frustrated
Appetites, for which you slam a door.
For sex should retain its adolescent shyness,
Shouldn't it?
               Or better to meet at sea,
Two dark gunboats that thump & shoot fire
All night, trying hard not to win.

These refusals begin to look like courage.
You're trying hard not to give in.

But you can't come down from yourself;
You wouldn't if you could.
So you end up speechless, writing it down:
That tapping all night is yourself.
    Mornings you wake up listless;
How could you choose this life, & how
Among friends, deny kindness? You keep your eye
At death—or death's abyss;
You never choose to drop.

Sometimes you refuse to put up with yourself
But you go on talking,
Thinking, maneuvering
Over the dark & chartless waters
& under mysterious orders not to come in.

Exile

*. . . the exile that belongs to oneself,
the interior exile.*
            —Richard Howard

We must have some statement from it, for now
We are keeping smaller ones, circumspect,

As when a man in the midst of self-argument
Turns bitterly aside. The countenance

Lost in itself will languish awhile,
As if memory were a buoyancy stunned,

Then sink. He begins a descent, as into
Experience—his inner space, or solitude.

Nothing so private as this resting place.
From it the heart rises, a red

Wet planet contracting in space
As if in pain or opposition to itself.

Meanwhile we, in a weak external light,
Infer second thought; or if unsure,

We assume his sudden distancing
Complementary to our own. Thus friendship

Like the moon releases its pull
& we slide back into our own lives.

Wrongly inspired by the indifference we assume,
Is it possible our lives, sustained

At last only by deep concentration
& by the conversations we fear might be running down,

Can be understood? Formerly we noticed experience.
It did not accurately repeat,

But our latest responses are now generalized.
Eventually we choose exile

& self-descent. If that inner universe,
Objective & in distant accord, affords some patience

Sometimes we see a man emerge, wholly himself.
Or ourselves choose love, a kind

Of concealment
So private we can hardly speak.

Level

You were of a certain age where the days are interchangeable.
Where formerly you had suffered introspection, & emerged,
& where formerly you had married, living a popular novel,
Now you were calm, though unsure, believing this calm
To be inconsolable, a long plain of ennui or private joy.

You had turned back momentarily then, though
To your surprise from concern rather than shock,
To settle a few things & acquaint yourself one last time.
Then as you embarked, as onto a flat field of water
Stepping lightly off, you remembered a foreshadowing:
An image of adults talking quietly in the backyard
& smoking, the evening a pale haze around their bodies.

Now that image in its familiarity takes care of you.
Another surprise: courage is not a requirement,
Because this new expansiveness, seeming always
To be a living extension of itself, only requires
Your presence; the slight pressure of your body.

But it is not all reassuring, this comfort,
For you belong to it. The world, & your small love for it,
Floats like the talk of the adults, & is barely mutable:
Now you will feel a nostalgia for it;
No longer will you consciously alter its events.

And friendship, & companionship, faces of young students
Which after the immediate pleasures of consent
Had settled into composure, always refreshing your life,
Must change value now; will be less quick & lovelier.
After a long time & if you again become articulate
Or can listen generously, it can be given to you
To be provident, though this is at the mercy of time
Among other dependencies, & is not assured.

The Edge

You rise each day, you make
Your little rounds, you sleep.

You rise to the edge of grief.
You fall at the edge of sleep.

A woman lies down, she smiles
Above her troubles, she sleeps.

You rise to the edge of appetite.
You fall at the edge of sleep.

A man lies down, his hand
Shadows his face, he sleeps.

You rise to the edge of his wound.
You fall at the edge of sleep.

You lie awake, you watch
The stars revolve, repeat.

You rise to the edge of the world.
You sleep, & then you sleep.

In Sepia

Often you walked at night, house lights made
    Nets of their lawns, your shadow
Briefly over them. You had been talking about
    Death, over & over. Often
You felt dishonest, though certainly some figure
    Moved in the dark yards, a parallel
Circumstance, keeping pace. By Death, you meant
    A change of character: He is
A step ahead, interlocutor, by whose whisper
    The future parts like water,

Allowing entrance. That was a way of facing it
    & circumventing it: Death
Was the person into whom you stepped. Life, then,
    Was a series of static events;
As: here the child, in sepia, climbs the front steps
    Dressed for winter. Even the snow
Is brown, &, no, he will never enter that house
    Because each passage, as into
A new life, requires his forgetfulness. Often you
    Would explore these photographs,

These memories, in sepia, of another life.
    Their use was tragic,
Evoking a circumstance, the particular fragments
    Of an always shattered past.
Death was process then, a release of nostalgia
    Leaving you free to change.
Perhaps you were wrong; but walking at night
    Each house got personal. Each
Had a father. He was reading a story so hopeless,
    So starless, we all belonged.

Stories

*. . . as in old journals, we come upon a story
that seems our own, and speaks, then passes.*

This is a story declining, as landscape
    Into its elements.
You saw that, driving through the midwest:

How at twilight certain trees, houses
    You pass, float
On a flat expansiveness—such plain

Seclusive bodies as the stages of memory
    That darken & go by.
Finally not much will have happened:

Some processions you can remember awhile
    Between which the land
Goes on, gliding without force toward
    Night & sleep.

*

You were telling a story. The story
    You lived was not
The same, though both had a loveliness

Which was years. And in the middle years
    You lost your way.
All winter the rain fell evenly down

& spring was mild. Evenings you took
    Your time, walking,
Coming home. What couples you passed

Talked quietly; bodies incomplete by dark,
    Hands touching, they
Glided by. The stars turned slowly
    Their exclusive joy.

*

From your neighbor the night divides you,
    & from yourself.
There was a dark, exclusive joy: the past.

All you had earned was passage. Fixed
    Points, by which
You measured time, a gradual lassitude

Had overcome. You accustomed yourself
    To the night. By
Lamplight, or firelight, you read

Yourself to sleep. These were your dreams:
    The steady motions
Of ships or seasons, by which disquietude
    You woke & read.

*

You had forgotten the words you wanted to say.
    I think you lay
Too often on a woman's breast. Now you were

Like those women who gathered on the shore
    Watching the ships;
Those heroes, their husbands, rose distantly

& dissolved. All of your constancy, now,
    Was only longing.
Most of it speechless, though often you wrote

Long letters, specific & even-toned, filled
     With ambiguous yearnings
For the absolute. You wrote about your work,
     Your wife, your home.

                    *

How can I say this, only beginning to see
     Such understanding as
Can make you whole. These stories end, as

Always, in our gradual belief. They are
     The lands we live in,
The women we finally meet as friends,

The friends we overcome. We overcome
     Ourselves. The words
You wanted are that story we tell

Ourselves so often it is eventually real
     Or plain; so, much
The same measure, or passing of time,
     Where we dissolve.

Years

Sometimes in weariness I stop.
Because I've been lucky
I think the future must be plain.
Over the trees the stars are quite small.

My friends talk quietly
& we have all come to the same things.
Now if I die, I will
Inherit awhile their similar bodies.

Now if I listen
Someone is telling a story.
The characters met.
They enchanted each other by speech.

Though the stories they lived
Were not the same,
Many were distracted into love,
Slept, & woke alone, awhile serene.

PITT POETRY SERIES

Colophon

The poems in this volume are set in Linotype Baskerville, a type which has survived for generations in spite of continuous "improvements." The display type on the title page is a Victorian exercise named Kismet, popular around 1900. The printing is by letterpress from the type, which was destroyed upon completion of the press run. The design is by Gary Gore.